COLORING
for Grown-Ups
HOLIDAY FUN BOOK

P

A PLUME BOOK

COLORING
for Grown-Ups
HOLIDAY FUN BOOK

Written and Illustrated by

Ryan Hunter & Taige Jensen

PLUME
Published by Penguin Group
Penguin Group (USA) LLC
375 Hudson Street
New York, New York 10014

USA | Canada | UK | Ireland | Australia | New Zealand | India | South Africa | China
penguin.com
A Penguin Random House Company

First published by Plume, a member of Penguin Group (USA) LLC, 2013

P REGISTERED TRADEMARK—MARCA REGISTRADA

ISBN 978-0-14-218068-6

Printed in the United States of America
10 9 8 7 6 5 4 3

Coloring for Grown-Ups
HOLIDAY FUN BOOK

MATERIALS NEEDED:

☐ Coloring utensils   ☐ Scissors

OPTIONAL:

☐ Awkward family interactions   ☐ Seasonal depression

☐ An excuse for day drinking   ☐ Weird uncles

☐ Unreliable Wi-Fi   ☐ Food coma/diarrhea

A brand-new year of holiday fun and learning awaits.
But first, you'll need to turn the page and figure out...

WHERE AM I, WHO IS THIS, AND HOW DO I LEAVE?

Use your imagination to gracefully escape the home of the stranger you slept with on New Year's Eve!

New Year's Day

NEW YEAR'S DAY WALK-OF-SHAME MAZE

How much shame can YOU avoid? Stop at the deli across the street for a hangover cure, the pharmacy for a pair of sunglasses, and the STD clinic to schedule an emergency appointment. Just try not to run into your ex, or any judgmental-looking strangers!

START

DELI

CLINIC

PHARMACY

FINISH
sleeping in your own bed!

New Year's Day

3

NEW YEAR'S DAY ACTIVITY FUN PAGE

ACTIVITY #1: Self-reflection

Begin by taking a good, hard look at yourself in the mirror, then report your findings on the right. Be sure not to leave out any bags under your eyes, day-old makeup, expressions of nausea and regret, or ill-advised facial tattoos!

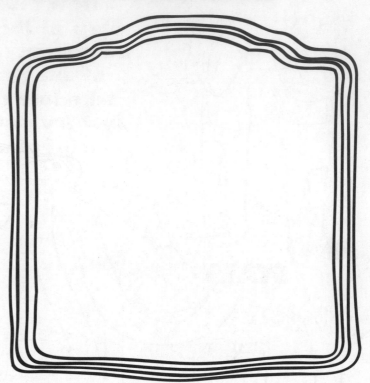

ACTIVITY #2: Enduring life changes

Connect the New Year's resolution to the caveat you will add to it next week.

LOSE WEIGHT	AT SOME POINT
QUIT SMOKING	IN PUBLIC
GET ORGANIZED	AROUND CHILDREN
DRINK LESS	IF I HAVE TIME
HELP OTHERS	WHEN ON CAMERA
BE MORE SEXUALLY RESPONSIBLE	SORT OF
GET A JOB	PRIOR TO ARMAGEDDON

HOLIDAY QUIZ

SPOOKY GHOST

LEPRECHAUN

CUPID

JESUS

EASTER BUNNY

UNCLE SAM

YOUR PARENTS' LOVE

GOOD WILL TOWARD MEN

SANTA

Circle all of the holiday symbols you no longer believe in!

(Then turn to page 55 to see how you did!)

DRAW DR. MARTIN LUTHER KING JR.'S DREAM!

Is he dreaming about a world united in racial harmony? Or getting chased by a gigantic pair of scissors? In dreams, anything is possible!

Martin Luther King Jr. Day

JUDGE THESE PEOPLE NOT BY THE COLOR OF THEIR SKIN, BUT BY THE CONTENT OF THEIR CHARACTER!

JUDGMENT: _____

_____

JUDGMENT: _____

_____

JUDGMENT: _____

_____

JUDGMENT: _____

_____

(Solutions on page 55)

Martin Luther King Jr. Day

CELEBRATE CHINESE NEW YEAR BY COLORING THE CHINESE PERSON

(Remember, there are Koreans, Japanese, Filipinos, and other Asian races on this page!)

Only color the Chinese person!

IN AN EFFORT TO HELP HIM SEE HIS SHADOW, SOMEBODY GAVE PUNXSUTAWNEY PHIL FOUR HITS OF PCP. NOW HE'S SEEING LOTS OF SHIT! DRAW HIS HALLUCINATIONS.

Groundhog Day

VALENTINES FOR GROWN-UPS

♡ I TOLERATE YOU ♡

To: _____ From: _____

WE'RE GETTING FAT

To: _____ From: _____

I'VE DECIDED TO START FARTING IN FRONT OF YOU

To: _____ From: _____

♡ MY PENIS ASKED ME TO GIVE YOU THIS ♡

To: _____ From: _____

Valentine's Day

10

VALENTINES FOR GROWN-UPS

♡ WE HAVE THE SAME STD ♡
SO YOU MIGHT AS WELL
STAY WITH ME FOR A WHILE

To: _____ From: _____

LOVE
IS A CONSTRUCT

I don't believe in valentines.

To: _____ From: _____

SOMEDAY YOU'LL LEARN
TO LIKE NICE GUYS...

You bitch.

To: _____ From: _____

♡ SO I GUESS
WE'RE DATING NOW? ♡

To: _____ From: _____

Valentine's Day

Help Abe & George commemorate their special day by finding 6 other famous presidents hidden around this mattress store!

President's Day

WHO WILL NEVER BE PRESIDENT?

Color which minority groups our freedom-loving nation will never, ever accept in a top position of leadership.

Latino **Woman** **Muslim** **Homosexual**

Mormon **Atheist** **Lizard person** **Bald guy**

(Solutions on page 55)

President's Day

HAPPY MARDI GRAS!
What did they show to get those beads?

YOU DECIDE!

ST. PATRICK'S DAY
PUKE-BY-NUMBERS
Follow the trail of multicolored vomit to help you locate this alcoholic little person's secret treasure!

St. Patrick's Day

ST. PATRICK'S DAY
FIND THE DIFFERENCES

Can you find 7 differences
between the image above and the one below?

(Solutions on page 55)

CONSPIRACY THEORY CONNECT-THE-DOTS

Use this marijuana to help you connect the dots between each of these "unrelated" events and figures. Report your conclusions below.

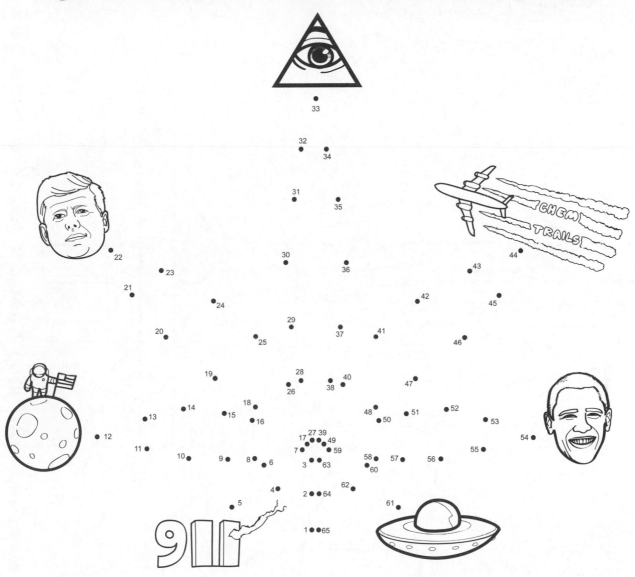

Conclusions: _____

_____

_____

Someone accidentally scheduled the Easter egg hunt on Good Friday!
Find all 7 eggs before Jesus notices this egg-regious mistake!

Help Jeshua Cottontail, the animal messiah, by drawing in his 12 animal apostles.

"This chocolate is my body. Consume it in remembrance of me, and ye shall have delicious, eternal life."
FooFoo 26:13

Easter

DRESS UP THIS TOTAL STRANGER AS YOUR FAVORITE HOLIDAY MALL MASCOT!

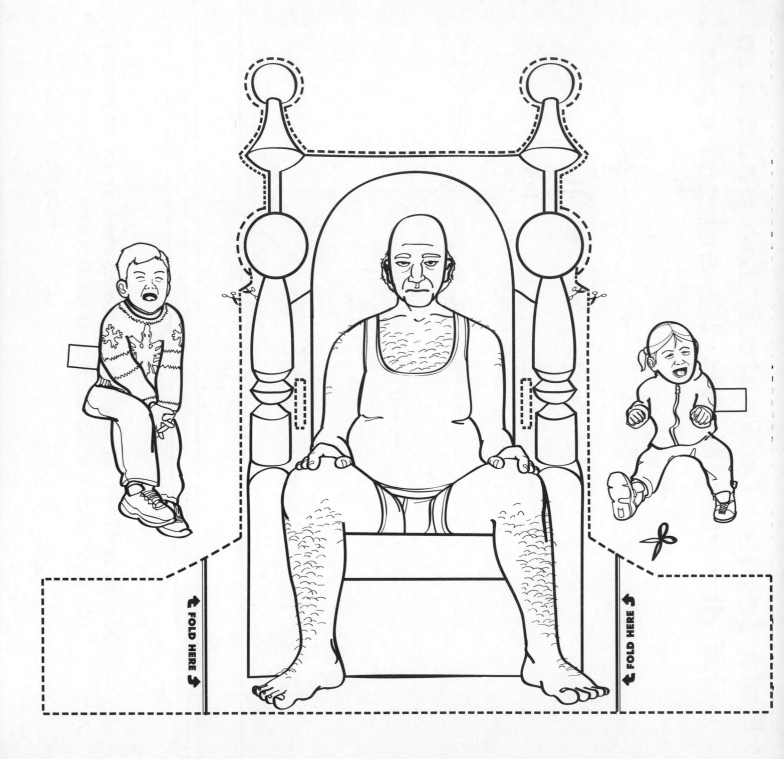

FOLD HERE

FOLD HERE

Christmas

Halloween

Easter

Which lap will YOU choose?

HAPPY EARTH DAY

Make Earth's day by imagining the various ways the human race might wipe itself off the face of the planet.

Earth Day

COLOR THESE LESSER-KNOWN HOLIDAY MASCOTS!

ASHY WENDY

The preachy pile of cinders!
(ASH WEDNESDAY)

MATZOH MAN

The guy who is a little too eager to tell everyone he's keeping kosher
(PASSOVER)

DOUGLAS FIR

Literally just a Douglas fir
(ARBOR DAY)

SANTA FE

The Mexican Santa
(CINCO DE MAYO)

WAIT...
TODAY WAS MOTHER'S DAY?

Quick! Draw something nice and e-mail it to her before she regrets bringing you into existence!

Mother's Day

MOTHER'S DAY GUILT QUILT

Contemplate the harrowing things your mother underwent to birth and raise you by adding YOUR mom's square to the quilt.

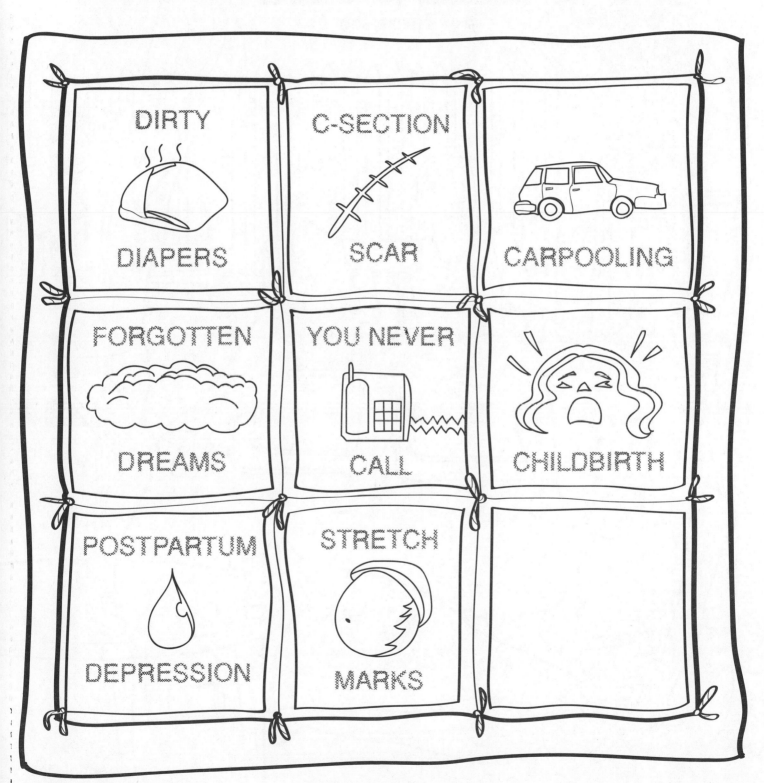

DIRTY DIAPERS

C-SECTION SCAR

CARPOOLING

FORGOTTEN DREAMS

YOU NEVER CALL

CHILDBIRTH

POSTPARTUM DEPRESSION

STRETCH MARKS

Mother's Day

REMEMBERING THE SERVICEMEN...
BY FORGETTING THE WEEKEND

Use a black marker to physically "black out" any memories you'd rather not hang on to.

Memorial Day

PRETEND TO BE JEWISH!

It's a beautiful day outside!
Using the syllables below, make up your own
Jewish holiday so your boss will let you ditch work!

rosh   hash   kip   shem   tov

vah

kew   mitz   maz   sim   yom

ziv   el

pah   tor

schmutz   chutz   suk

oy

sha   vey   schmear   lom

pur

Mr. Wagoner

Today is definitely:

Miscellaneous Jewish Holiday

Draw the son your father hoped you'd be!

WORD SEARCH
FOR YOUR DAD'S APPROVAL

```
E L P Y W U E D N Q E T U F K L Z C V T
B R J T U N W Y K E B H O A I D N H J H
Y K C J D E M B A R R A S S M E N T W V
S B O G S B F P R W S J O I G K R F S D
M N T F G I D I O T M E F M L T Q E C I
N D E A M W L B K O D R A G A N L I R S
U J W I L O V E Y O U K I D D O A J E A
A H G L D R E L U W A T L A Y E Z A W B
R C I U P T Y I M P R O U D O F Y O U M
R E N R R H R E T A R D R Y U B E T P O
E X T E S L Y V O K E S E O E J L X G I
R I M T H E R E F O R Y O U X H V I D N
I E O Y U S E I B D S T U P I D I R E T
A S R D J S L N N J A C K A S S V L G M
V Y O U R E M Y F A V O R I T E E M Y E
E S N M F I Y O A R E S P S L A I Y N N
N F J M L R P U T Z N Y W U E D N Q U T
X W R Y I A D G J L X V N Q R Y U O F V
```

WORD BANK: There isn't one.
Word banks are for children and the weak.

NEED HELP?
All 6 solutions can be found on page 57, aka "the Quitter's Page."

HAPPY INDEPENDENCE DAY!

China just bought the rights to "The Star-Spangled Banner"! Hurriedly pen a new national anthem to motivate and inspire the American people!

We've started it for you.

Oh, _____ freedom
_____
liberty _____
_____ ramparts
_____
majesty _____ spangled
_____
_____
#1 _____ America
_____
flag _____ the best
_____

Independence Day

HAPPY LABOR DAY!
Celebrate the economic and social contributions of workers by drawing what you plan to do with your latest unemployment check.

Labor Day

COLOR THESE LESSER-KNOWN HOLIDAY MASCOTS!

HOT BETSY ROSS

Great seamstress; SICK body, bro

(FLAG DAY)

MUGGSY

The lying mug!

(FATHER'S DAY)

LABOR DAVE

Everyone's favorite non-Mexican laborer

(LABOR DAY)

JOSH HASHANAH

Chill harbinger of the Jewish New Year

(ROSH HASHANAH)

HAPPY COLUMBUS DAY, AMERICA!

Help Christopher Columbus navigate the dangerous waters of the Atlantic Ocean so he can discover the New World and safely deliver cholera to the natives.

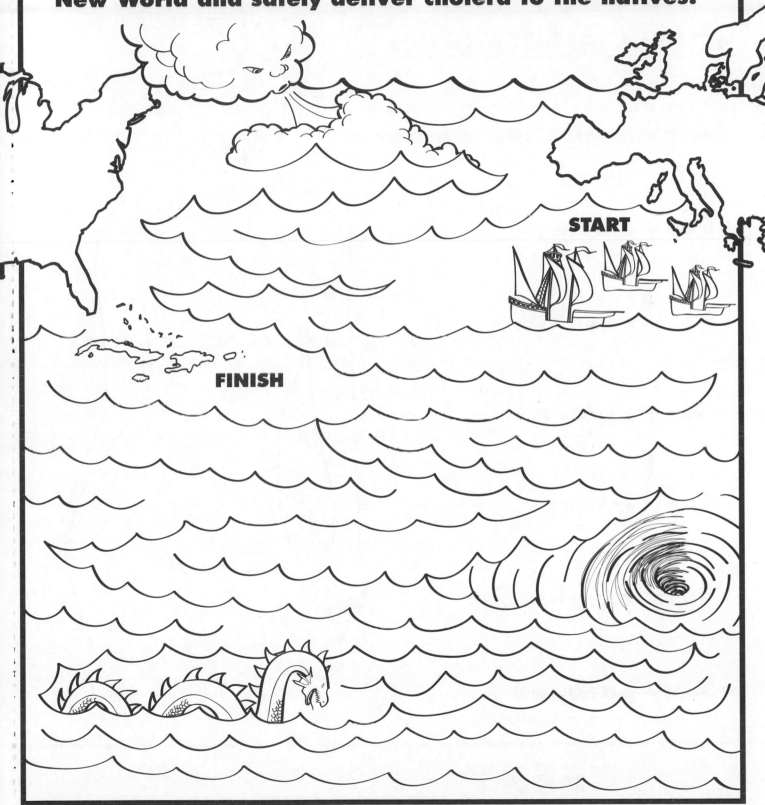

CONSTRUCT YOUR OWN:
SLUTTY HALLOWEEN COSTUME!

HELPFUL SUGGESTIONS:

- **Sexy sanitation worker**

- **Sexy clown**

- **Sexy roadkill**

- **Sexy notary**

- **Sexy infant**

- **Sexy taxidermist**

- **Sexy garbage**

"SEXY _____"

IT'S HALLOWEEN! You've decided to stay inside this year and be haunted by your inner demons. Color yours below!

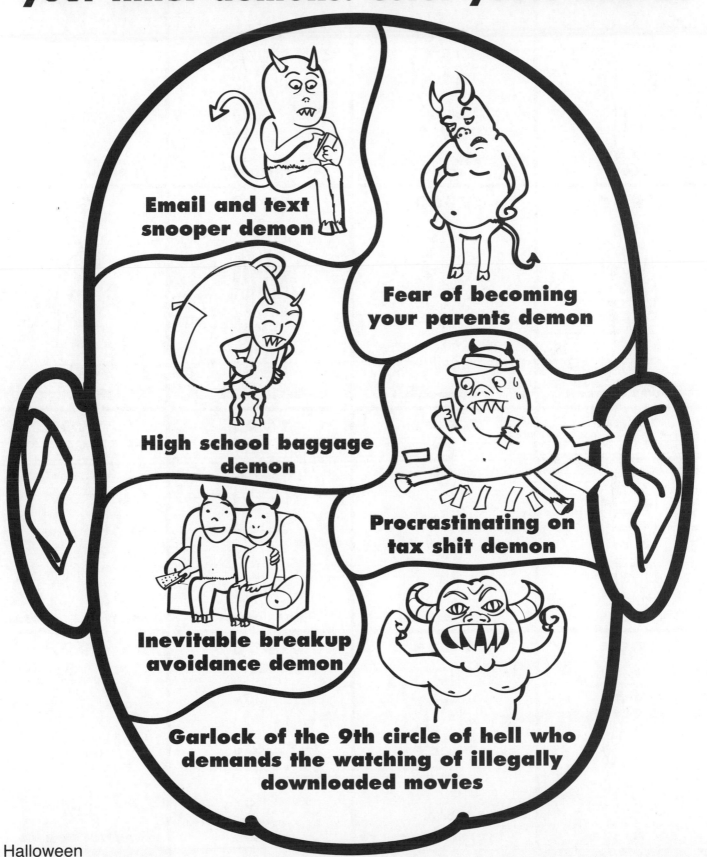

Email and text snooper demon

Fear of becoming your parents demon

High school baggage demon

Procrastinating on tax shit demon

Inevitable breakup avoidance demon

Garlock of the 9th circle of hell who demands the watching of illegally downloaded movies

HALLOWEEN

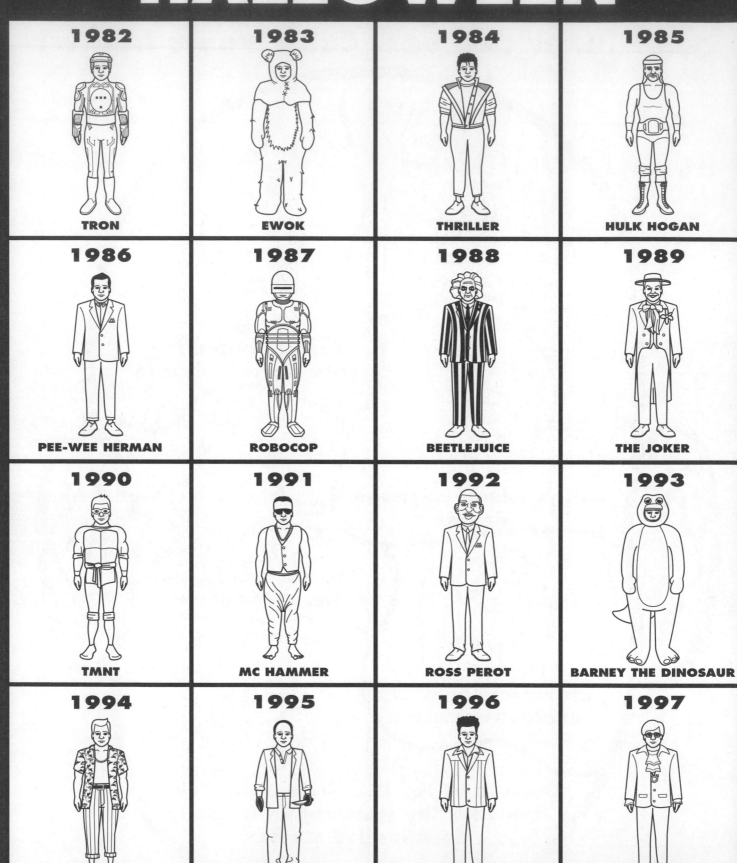

COLOR THE ZEITGEIST!

HALL OF FAME

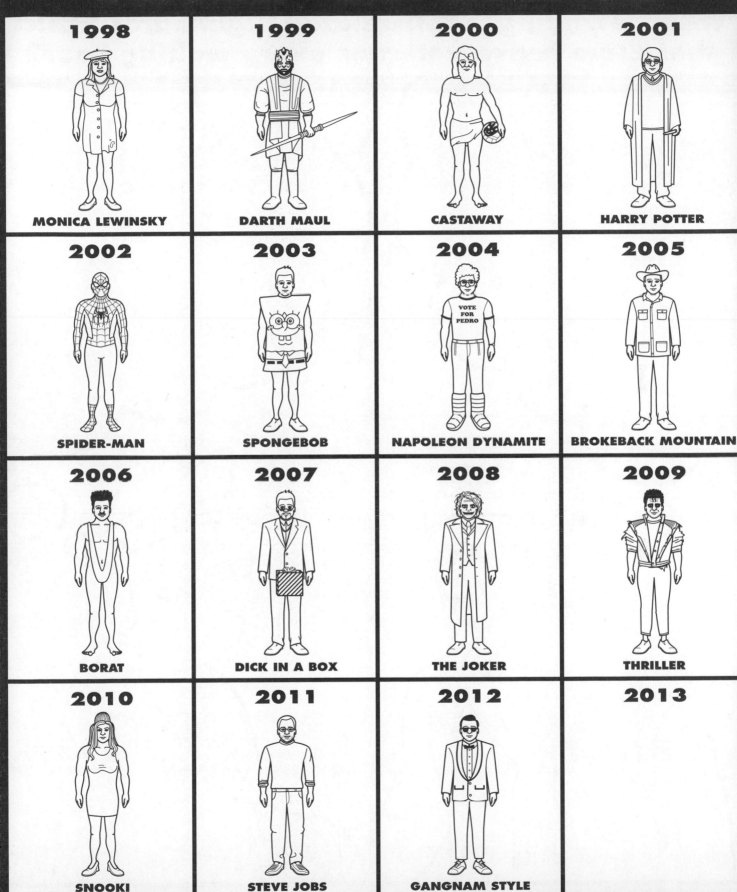

1998 — MONICA LEWINSKY

1999 — DARTH MAUL

2000 — CASTAWAY

2001 — HARRY POTTER

2002 — SPIDER-MAN

2003 — SPONGEBOB

2004 — NAPOLEON DYNAMITE

2005 — BROKEBACK MOUNTAIN

2006 — BORAT

2007 — DICK IN A BOX

2008 — THE JOKER

2009 — THRILLER

2010 — SNOOKI

2011 — STEVE JOBS

2012 — GANGNAM STYLE

2013

COMPLETE THE ZEITGEIST!

HAPPY VETERANS DAY!
What terrifying, PTSD-related nightmares afflict these two brave veterans every waking hour?

"THANKS."

In gratitude for helping him survive the winter, this pilgrim wants to teach his Indian friend about his own expertise: unnecessary buckles and shame.

Help them become best friends forever by drawing six unnecessary buckles in locations of your own choosing.

Thanksgiving

TRY NOT TO LOOK AT YOUR PHONE!

Thanksgiving

COLOR THESE LESSER-KNOWN HOLIDAY MASCOTS!

ERIG

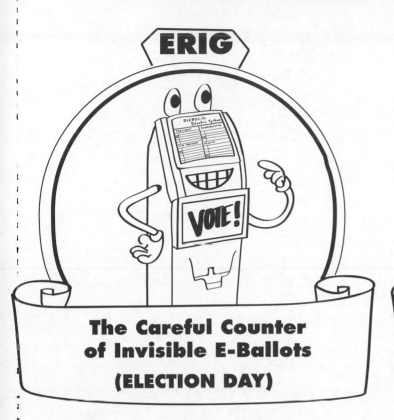

The Careful Counter of Invisible E-Ballots

(ELECTION DAY)

THE TRAMPLER

The heroic union of capitalism and Darwinism

(BLACK FRIDAY)

NO-PANTS NED

The casual shopper

(CYBER MONDAY)

HANUKKLAUS

Eight times the man Santa will ever be

(HANUKKAH)

PEARL HARBOR REMEMBRANCE DAY

MAY 25, 2001

Pearl Harbor Day

THE CHOSEN PEOPLE

Illustrate how Jews light up the world by lighting up this menorah with the faces of your 8 favorite Jews!

JEW BANK:

Jeff Goldblum	Carl Sagan	Natalie Portman	Ruth Bader Ginsburg
Anne Frank	Lena Dunham	Moses	Sandy Koufax
Noam Chomsky	Elie Wiesel	Golda Meir	Ben Stiller
Carrie Fisher	Drake	Magneto	Mark Zuckerberg
Barney Frank	Larry David	Jesus Christ	...OR PICK YOUR OWN!

Hanukkah

WHAT DID SANTA DO WITH HIS 364 VACATION DAYS?

Draw your findings above.

SANTA'S LITTLE HELPERS!

Dress these toy-making underage sweatshop workers like festive Christmas elves!

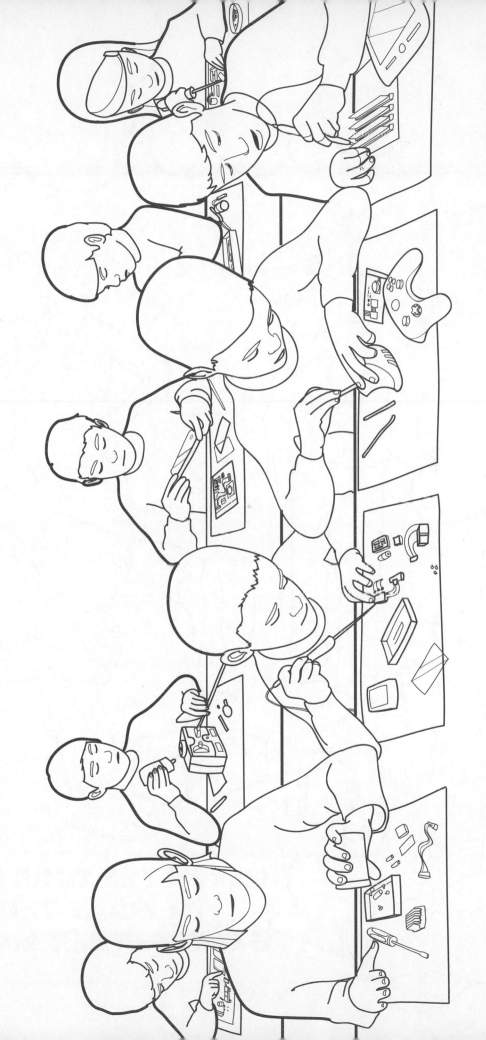

FILL IN THE THOUGHT BUBBLES TO MAKE THIS FAMILY GET-TOGETHER MORE HONEST!

Christmas

DESIGN YOUR OWN IRONICALLY HIDEOUS HOLIDAY SWEATER!

Winter Holiday Season

IS THIS A SNOWMAN, SNOWWOMAN, OR SNOWTRANSGENDER?

We won't know until you draw in some frosty white genitals.

Winter Holiday Season

Santa is only legally permitted to use his telepathic mind powers on children. But he still remembers the naughtiest thing you ever did.

And he'll never forget it...

Christmas

FIND THE HIDDEN MEANING
OF CHRISTMAS!

ADVENT	GIFTS	NUTCRACKER	STAR
ANGEL	GINGERBREAD	ORNAMENTS	STOCKING
BOWS	GIVING	PRESENTS	TINSEL
CARDS	HYMNS	REINDEER	TOY
CAROLING	LIGHTS	ROOFTOP	TREE
CHIMNEY	MISTLETOE	RUDOLPH	WINTER
ELF	MYRRH	SHOPPING	WISH
FROSTY	NOEL	SLEIGH	WREATH
GARLAND	NORTH POLE	SNOW	YULE LOGS

```
O G B R F P M U M W H E N K A M G F P O P
R A J A Q E I N Y I T C O V F G I X K R S
O D Y B O W S A R N I A G I R B V W Y G U
R V W R E A T H R T N C A R O L I N G B D
N E R U D O L P H E S T O C K I N G W E O
S N O W T R E E P R E S E N T S G I I M L
X T O C O N T S U M L E R U I S M N S R P
G I F T S G O R N A M E N T S L I G H T S
B H T O Y A E L F M A N O C H S L E I G H
S N O E L R E I N D E E R R O C A R D S T
N C P Y U L E L O G S H T A P H N B F O R
V Q A N D A F R O S T Y H C P I G R G D E
E I X G T N U T P F A M P K I M E E T N R
B A F U R D I N O T R N O E N N L A I L E
C V B P M H S D X J I S L R G E T D P K Q
H S O N E U Q V A G B Z E B S Y Z H O W J
```

DON'T FORGET TO READ BETWEEN THE LINES!
(Solutions on page 57)

CONNECT THESE RE-GIFTS TO THEIR NEW RECIPIENTS!

Be careful not to give them to the original giver!

(Solutions on page 57)

HELP BRIAN APPEASE HIS WHITE GUILT BY MATCHING EACH WORD TO THE CORRECT KWANZAA SYMBOL!

KINARA

MZEKA

MAZAO

MUHINDI

KIKOMBE CHA UMOJA

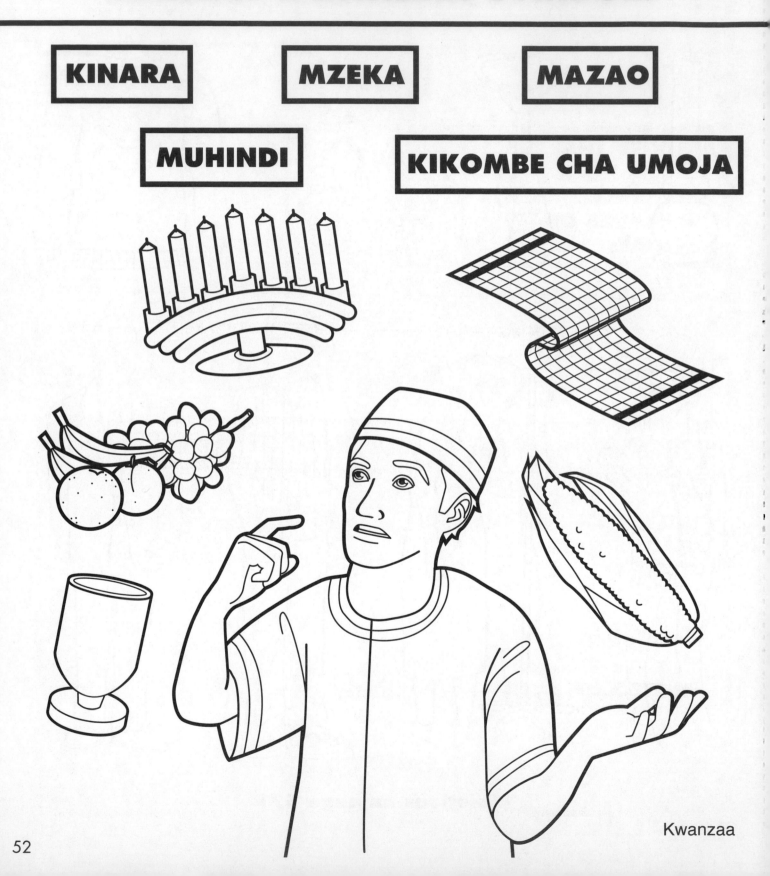

Kwanzaa

DESIGN YOUR OWN FEDERAL HOLIDAY!

HOLIDAY NAME:

DATE(S) OBSERVED:

ACTIVITY THAT IS TRADITIONALLY PARTICIPATED IN BY OBSERVERS OF THIS HOLIDAY:

UNIQUE SYMBOL, LOGO, OR IMAGE MOST ASSOCIATED WITH THIS HOLIDAY:

ACTIVITY THAT IS EXPRESSLY FORBIDDEN DURING THE OBSERVANCE OF THIS HOLIDAY:

WACKY, IMPRACTICAL HAT WORN IN PUBLIC TO DEMONSTRATE HOLIDAY ZEAL:

MINORITY GROUP THAT THIS HOLIDAY (circle one) CELEBRATES, EXPLOITS, OPPRESSES, OR DEMEANS:

THIS HOLIDAY'S WELL-KNOWN MOTTO OR SONG:

THIS HOLIDAY'S PECULIAR BUT BELOVED MASCOT OR FIGUREHEAD:

53

RESOLUTION RECAP

It's excuse-making time. Match each New Year's resolution to the holiday (or holidays) that prevented you from keeping it!

Eat healthier/ lose weight

Drink less

Get out of debt

Quit smoking

Be less stressed

Get along better with loved ones

Be more sexually responsible

NEW YEAR'S

VALENTINE'S DAY

ST. PATRICK'S DAY

INDEPENDENCE DAY

HALLOWEEN

THANKSGIVING

CHRISTMAS

New Year's Eve

54

SOLUTIONS

HOLIDAY QUIZ

P. 5

SANTA · CUPID · LEPRECHAUN · SPOOKY GHOST

GOOD WILL TOWARD MEN · UNCLE SAM · EASTER BUNNY · JESUS · YOUR PARENTS' LOVE

Circle all of the holiday symbols you no longer believe in!

(Then turn to page 55 to see how you did!)

What is your emotional maturity level?
Award yourself 1 point for each symbol you circled

0 points - toddler	1 - 5 points - child
6 points - adolescent	7 points - adult
8 points - Übermensch	9 points - major dick

ST. PATRICK'S DAY FIND THE DIFFERENCES

Can you find 7 differences between the image above and the one below?

P. 16

1. Totally different bro — that's Corey. (The guy before was Tobey.)
2. The girl you're talking to does not actually look like this.
3. The room is pulsating. Always a good sign.
4. It's night-time? Jesus.
5. Impending life mistake.
6. Former BFF throwdown.
7. THAT'S Tobey.
Also, either the clock is broken or you've been drinking for literally twelve hours. Please seek help.

JUDGE THESE PEOPLE NOT BY THE COLOR OF THEIR SKIN, BUT BY THE CONTENT OF THEIR CHARACTER!

JUDGMENT: _____

JUDGMENT: _____

JUDGMENT: _____

JUDGMENT: _____

P. 7

1. The woman in the top left was actually pushing that elderly woman into traffic. She remains at large.
2. The man in the top right was trying to talk a casual acquaintance down from a suicide attempt.
3. The guy robbing the bank talks more than he listens but is a dependable friend and will totally help you move if you need it.
4. The guy on the unicycle knows who the Zodiac Killer was and never told anyone.

Maybe next time don't be so judgmental?

WHO WILL NEVER BE PRESIDENT?

Color which minority groups our freedom-loving nation will never, ever accept in a top position of leadership.

Latino · Woman · Muslim · Homosexual

Mormon · Atheist · Lizard person · Bald guy

P. 13

This page was a trick question. A lizard person is always president.

COUPONS FOR GROWN-UPS

GOOD FOR ONE FULL DAY OF LOOKING AT YOU WHILE YOU TALK INSTEAD OF AT TECHNOLOGY.

GIVER: _____

RECIPIENT: _____

ColoringForGrownups.com

GOOD FOR ONE WEEK WHERE I DON'T SECRETLY USE YOUR SHAMPOO.

(I'VE BEEN SECRETLY USING YOUR SHAMPOO.)

GIVER: _____

RECIPIENT: _____

ColoringForGrownups.com

GOOD FOR ONE ACT OF COMPLICITY IN THE LIE OF YOUR CHOICE.

GIVER: _____

RECIPIENT: _____

ColoringForGrownups.com

GET-OUT-OF-HOLIDAY FREE CARD

GOOD FOR THE FORGETTING OR BLOWING-OFF OF ONE SUPPOSEDLY IMPORTANT CULTURAL RITUAL

GIVER: _____

RECIPIENT: _____

ColoringForGrownups.com

SOLUTIONS

WORD SEARCH
FOR YOUR DAD'S APPROVAL

WORD BANK: There isn't one.
Word banks are for children and the weak.

P.S. Because you had to look in the back, all of the above no longer applies.

CONNECT THESE RE-GIFTS TO THEIR NEW RECIPIENTS!
Be careful not to give them to the original giver!

1. Your recently divorced uncle Ken gave you the bong so you would want to hang out with him. Give it to your grandma to help her with her tumors.

2. Your boss gave you a cheap tie because he doesn't want you to know that he hates you. Give it to Uncle Ken to equip him for the custody hearing he will ultimately be too stoned to attend.

3. Your neighbor Misty gave you the sexy handcuffs, because she's unstable and has trouble with personal boundaries. Anonymously give these to your boss as a coded threat about reporting him to the SEC. (He'll totally get it.)

4. Grandma gave you the cat sweater because she has tumors and thought it would be a good idea. Give it to your neighbor Misty to effectively squelch any and all sexual tension. That stupid sweater just saved your life!

FIND THE HIDDEN MEANING OF CHRISTMAS!

ADVENT	GIFTS	NUTCRACKER	STAR
ANGEL	GINGERBREAD	ORNAMENTS	STOCKING
BOWS	GIVING	PRESENTS	TINSEL
CARDS	HYMNS	REINDEER	TOY
CAROLING	LIGHTS	ROOFTOP	TREE
CHIMNEY	MISTLETOE	RUDOLPH	WINTER
ELF	MYRRH	SHOPPING	WISH
FROSTY	NOEL	SLEIGH	WREATH
GARLAND	NORTHPOLE	SNOW	YULELOGS

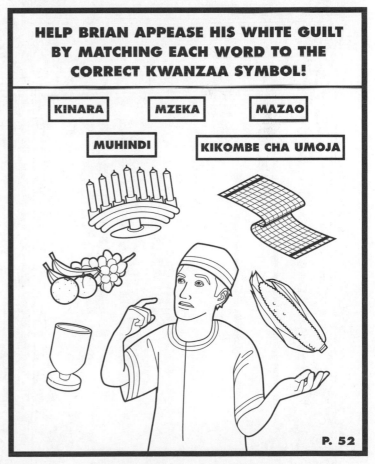

Or did we just blow your mind? Wake up, sheeple!

HELP BRIAN APPEASE HIS WHITE GUILT BY MATCHING EACH WORD TO THE CORRECT KWANZAA SYMBOL!

KINARA   MZEKA   MAZAO

MUHINDI   KIKOMBE CHA UMOJA

Just google it, you racist.

COUPONS FOR GROWN-UPS

GOOD FOR
ONE DAY THAT I
PROMISE NOT TO SAY OUT
LOUD HOW MUCH I HATE
EVERYTHING.

RECIPIENT: _____

GIVER: _____

ColoringForGrownups.com

GOOD FOR ONE
JUDGMENT-FREE
ORGANIZATION OF THE
PAPERWORK/UNOPENED MAIL
THAT IS RUINING YOUR LIFE.

RECIPIENT: _____

GIVER: _____

ColoringForGrownups.com

GOOD FOR ONE
CONSEQUENCE-FREE
BATSHIT-INSANE
MENTAL BREAKDOWN

RECIPIENT: _____

GIVER: _____

ColoringForGrownups.com

ONE COUPON TO
FORGET THIS EVER
HAPPENED.

RECIPIENT: _____

GIVER: _____

ColoringForGrownups.com

Credits

WRITTEN AND ILLUSTRATED BY
Ryan Hunter and Taige Jensen

ADDITIONAL ILLUSTRATIONS BY
Avery Monsen

CREATIVE TEAM

Aleks Arcabascio	Lexie Kahanovitz
Dan Avidan	Laura Lane
Zach Broussard	Jenn Lyon
Andrew Bush	Avery Monsen
Noah Byrne	Brent Schmidt
Anna Callegari	Achilles Stamatelaky
Dru Johnston	Adam D. Strauss

Acknowledgments

In addition to all the folks listed above, a big thanks to everybody at Penguin and Plume, especially Becky Cole, Kate Napolitano, and Lucy Kim. And another giant thank-you to the great Jason Allen Ashlock.

This is the second book we could not have made without the national treasure that is Jenn Lyon. We also had help from our friends Yahea Abdulla, Matthew Alston, Paul Briganti, Joseph Childers, Mike Force, Jonny Gillette, Tyler Jackson, Ryan Karels, Carlylia Muller, Lauren Reeves, Nick Rutherford, and Michael Swaim.

Finally, in our last book we said we wanted to thank our parents but planned to wait until we made a book that had less dicks in it. Speaking strictly from a numbers perspective, this is that book. So at long last—thank you to Gail and Joe Werner, Harry and Kerri Hunter, Carol Fox Olsen, and Dave and Jan Jensen. You made us, and we made this book. We're all sharing the blame on this one.

With love and sincerity,
Ryan & Taige

About the Authors

Taige Jensen and Ryan Hunter are a New York–based pair of writer-actor-filmmaker-author-illustrators. Their first book, *Coloring for Grown-Ups: The Adult Activity Book* is more or less exactly like this one, but with different words and pictures.

Their sketch comedy channel, POYKPAC, has garnered over 77 million views on YouTube. Follow them around the Internet:

@taige   @colorfulhumor   @ryan_hunter

poykpac.com   YouTube.com/POYKPAC   @POYKPAC

ColoringForGrownups.com   facebook.com/ColoringForGrownups

AUTHOR ILLUSTRATIONS BY SHEA SERRANO